THEM

THEY COME AT NIGHT

VOLUME 2

Compiled and rewritten
by
Tom Lyons

THEM: THEY COME AT NIGHT, VOLUME 2

Copyright © 2023 Tom Lyons

All rights reserved. No part of this may be reproduced without the author's prior consent, except for brief quotes used in reviews.

All information and opinions expressed in *Them: They Come at Night, Volume 2* are based upon the personal perspectives and experiences of those generous enough to submit them. Tom Lyons does not purport that the information presented in this book is based on accurate, current, or valid scientific knowledge.

Acknowledgments

It's certainly no easy task for people to discuss their encounters with the unknown. I want to thank the many good people who took the time and energy to put their experiences into writing.

A few of the following names were altered or replaced with "anonymous" to respect those involved.

Would you like to see your report in an issue of *Them: They Come at Night*?

If so, all you have to do is type up a summary of your experience and email it to Tom Lyons at:

Living.Among.Bigfoot@gmail.com

Special Offer

If your report gets accepted, you will receive an exclusive paperback copy signed by Tom shortly after the book is released. If you'd like to participate in that offer, please include your mailing address in the email.

Contents

Report #1 1

Report #2 38

Report #3 67

Report #4 74

Conclusion 95

Editor's Note 97

Mailing List Sign-Up Form 99

Social Media 101

About the Editor...103

THEM: They Come at Night, Volume 2

Report #1

I had always wanted to live in New York City since I was a little girl. Early dreams of becoming a fashion icon had made me determined to get there as soon as possible. However, how could I have anticipated the horror that accompanied that desire?

At age seventeen, I left my home in rural Iowa to pursue my fashion career. I didn't get along with my mom or her boyfriend, so there wasn't much incentive to stay. I always felt so restless in that state—like I was watching my life pass before my eyes. I never felt like I fit in that well with other kids in my area, for none of them seemed to have grand aspirations. It might come off as mean-spirited, but I had the feeling that they would end up in precisely the same place as their parents when we got older. It was like they were becoming more and more like their mom or dad by the day; that was very noticeable to me from a young age, and something about that terrified me.

Fortunately, I had a grandmother who was very encouraging about my decision to leave my hometown. She was the only one in my family who supported my destiny of becoming a fashion designer. She had also fled her hometown at a young age and said that was one of the better decisions she made, claiming that she wouldn't have matured so early had she not taken the risk. Discreetly, my grandma helped with my living costs and even gave me considerable money for fashion school. I tear up thinking about how supportive and generous that woman was.

To make a long story short, I encountered a girl at Central Park searching for someone to model for her school project. Coincidentally, she was a fashion student at the school I wanted to attend most of all. She introduced herself as Marceline, and we immediately clicked. She whipped out her portfolio to show me her latest designs, and I couldn't have been more ecstatic.

The friendship felt meant to be right from our introduction. But just when I thought things couldn't get any better, Marceline informed me that her roommate, who was also a student at her school, had recently dropped out and was leaving New York City. Within less than a week of meeting Marceline, I had become her new roommate, and she even paid more of the rent to make things easier for me. I learned she was from a wealthy family who assisted her with virtually everything. They also ended up putting in a good word for me at the school because they had connections to someone who was good friends with someone working in admissions, and I got accepted to enroll for the upcoming term.

I spent the next few days on cloud nine, wondering how I could've gotten so lucky. It felt like the stars were aligning in every way possible. The high-rise apartment was so much nicer than anything I had ever expected to live in, which made the already hard-to-believe situation that much more mesmerizing. But unfortunately, things started to feel weird when I witnessed a disturbing scene through someone else's apartment window.

Directly across the street from where we lived was a high-rise condominium, even fancier than the building we lived in. Although it looked like it could've been one of the oldest structures in New York, it also appeared to be one of the most well-maintained. There was no question that the traditional gothic architecture attracted a wide variety of the city's wealthiest residents.

Anyway, Marceline was out with some guy she had a crush on while I stayed home to get a head start on some new design sketches that I thought would come in handy once I started classes. I was sitting on the couch in the common room when something incredibly bizarre caught my eye across the way. I'm not sure how to put it other than to say I saw someone with green skin walk through the room. At first, I thought I had to have imagined it, but then I saw the same thing a few moments later—that time with a much longer-lasting view.

It wasn't a situation where there was a green tint to the lighting or anything like that; I could clearly see that the shirtless man had green, scalelike skin. I immediately got a bad feeling while looking at the individual; it felt like I was seeing something I shouldn't. Moments later, I saw them hunched over their kitchen table. They were turned away from me, but I could tell they were feasting upon something. His body twitched while they devoured whatever was in front of him, and watching that made me feel even more creeped out.

I'm not sure whether I might've imagined this aspect, but it looked to me like his torso expanded every few seconds before returning to normal. Perhaps that was a side effect of digestion; who can say? That routine seemed to persist until the scaly man finished his meal. Still, I couldn't see what was on that plate, as his back remained turned toward me after he rose to his feet and walked out of sight.

I remained in awe, trying to convince myself that I had imagined the whole thing. I can't emphasize enough how abrupt the sighting felt; I doubt there's any way that anyone could ever prepare themselves for something like it. That seems impossible. The sighting clashed with everything I thought to be possible, and it truly made me feel insecure. Although the scaly individual hadn't yet looked my way, I couldn't help but feel vulnerable to them. For whatever reason, it felt dangerous being anywhere near them—even with the thousands of other people occupying our buildings and the streets.

I finally rushed to close the blinds after I gained enough courage to stand up. I then returned to the couch and anxiously awaited Marceline's return. I tried to distract myself by working on my sketches, but that quickly proved futile.

When Marceline returned from her date night, she immediately commented on how I looked like I had seen a ghost. But she was a few drinks deep, which seemed to help her immediately move on to venting about drama involving the guy she had spent the evening with. I had to aggressively cut her off so that I could explain what I saw earlier that evening, and that marked the first time we got a little snappy with each other. But her condescending attitude faded as soon as she comprehended what I was talking about.

It turned out that Marceline had glimpsed similar things occurring in the same apartment across the way but had no idea who to tell. Additionally, she was worried that others would ridicule her over such a claim. Though we were both insecure about what others thought of us, I'd say that she was slightly more worried about that sort of thing. She was the type who never felt like she could leave home without spending at least an hour perfecting her makeup. I also liked to look presentable when out and about, but Marceline took it to another level. The more I got to know her, the more I realized she took pretty much every possible insecurity to another level, so, of course, she's not going to feel confident telling anyone about a supposed lizard man that lives across the street.

"I've seen that guy," she said. "My vision isn't the best from that distance, but it sometimes feels like he's looking at me. It's as if he knows I know his secret, and he's taunting me because he knows I can't do a thing about it."

I took a few moments to consider her words. Although I never caught the man looking at me, I could imagine him doing what Marceline mentioned. I had only just seen the guy, but he had this confident presence about him—like he wasn't the least bit worried about anyone watching him.

"So there really is a lizard man...," I muttered. "Wow, that's so weird."

"Lizard-man?" Marceline chuckled. "I think he's just some guy with a skin condition and doesn't mind sharing it with the world."

I wanted to consider her words seriously, but that was extremely difficult based on what I had seen earlier that night. I just knew something remarkably rare was occurring right across the busy city street.

Regardless of what Marceline believed about what we saw, we

gathered the courage to turn off our living room lights and then took another discreet peek at our neighbor's apartment. His blinds were down, so neither of us saw anything strange during the remainder of that night.

But only a few nights later, I woke up and had this random urge to walk toward my bedroom window and look outside. My eyes immediately landed on the odd-looking spine of the shirtless man. That was all I needed to confirm that Marceline's perspective wasn't entirely accurate. It couldn't have merely been a skin condition; what I saw looked like a different species.

Without hesitation, I ran toward my roommate's room, completely forgetting that she had a male guest over that night. When I popped my head into her room, Marceline shrieked out of embarrassment since she and her male friend were both nude and in the middle of an intimate act.

"What are you doing?" she screamed, diving under the blankets to cover herself. "Haven't you heard of knocking?"

"I'm so sorry!" I replied, likely even more humiliated than my roommate and her guy friend combined. "But you need to see this!"

I don't remember for sure, but I don't think the guy (who I hadn't yet met) said a word; he probably felt too awkward even to introduce himself.

When Marceline and I arrived at the window, we immediately saw one of the strangest sights of my life. The lizard-man was sitting at his dining room table, swinging his head from left to right with his arms extended across the table. He looked different than before; by that, I mean more reptilian.

Since her weak vision couldn't see the full extent of the visible features, I guess she needed me to confirm that they hadn't played tricks on her. With great detail, I informed her of everything I saw: the scaly skin, pointy spine, pronounced cheekbones, and cold-blooded eyes. I wouldn't go as far as to say that they looked like a lizard's eyes; it was just that the man looked like he wasn't in his right mind; it looked like something was bothering him—like he was stressed and going stir-crazy. My perception could've been wrong, but that's what it looked like to me at the time. Had it not been for the reptilian-like appearance, I would've assumed this individual was overdosing on amphetamines.

Marceline and I got caught up in a bit of a trance while trying to comprehend what we were looking at, and I nearly had a heart attack when she suddenly shrieked right next to me. The guy who had been in her room (and was now clothed) placed his hand on her shoulder while looking out the window. Her startled reaction nearly caused my heart to explode inside my chest.

"What are you guys looking at?" her friend asked just before apologizing to me for not having introduced himself earlier. He told me his name was John right before peering out the window and saying, "what's his problem?"

Marceline and I returned our attention to the building across the street and simultaneously shrieked. Our strange neighbor stood directly behind his window and stared into the eyes of all three of us. He didn't appear angry or happy; he seemed emotionless. Marceline rushed to close the blinds before we could continue the awkward staring contest.

"Who was that?" John said, beyond baffled.

"He's just some creepy neighbor," Marceline replied.

"Why was he staring at you guys without his shirt on?" John asked. I found it interesting that he hadn't mentioned anything about a lizard-like appearance, soon to recognize that the guy looked much more like a regular human while staring at us than at any other point I had seen him.

"I don't know," Marceline said, apparently annoyed that her guest demanded explanations for the abnormality. "Why don't you march over there and ask him yourself?"

John gulped at the suggestion; the look in his eyes expressed that he wasn't about to confront a guy he thought might be a serial killer. I certainly couldn't blame him for the blatant lack of confidence.

"Well, maybe you should report him to the police, don't you think?" John eventually replied.

"And what would we would tell the cops, exactly?" Marceline asked. "Should I explain that a man was looking out his window across the street and making eye contact with me?"

"Yeah, sure, I don't know," John said. "There must be something you can say to ensure he stays away. Tell them he gives you a bad feeling."

"You want me to tell the police I have a bad feeling? Really?" Marceline replied with a tone that implied her friend's advice was some of the stupidest she had ever heard. "I'm sure that'll work out well, especially in a hectic place like New York City."

"Well, we need to do something, don't you think?" John pleaded.

"I suppose you can go over there and knock on his door if you want?" Marceline sarcastically mentioned. "Maybe that'll scare him out of his wits, and he'll choose never to look in our direction again."

John looked unsure of what to say. He wanted to help but also didn't want to do anything that could put him in harm's way.

"Uh—," he stuttered.

"Oh, come on," Marceline said. "Pretty please, won't you do it for me?"

John walked out of the common room, and I assumed he was merely going to the bathroom. But it wasn't long after I started chatting with Marceline that we noticed he was halfway out the door.

"John, where are you going?" Marceline called out, but the door shut before she finished her sentence.

"He probably got upset that I called him out on his unwillingness to take care of things," she snickered. "But I'm sure he'll come crawling back before not too long."

We resumed our chat about the strange behavior across the street, occasionally and discreetly glancing toward the mysterious condo. It wasn't long before we noticed the unit's lights turn off. We didn't think much of it, assuming the guy had probably left home for a bit, and we continued talking about all sorts of stuff because Marceline had an awkward tendency to ramble.

Maybe fifteen minutes later, we noticed the lights switch back on, and we immediately saw the object hanging on the window. It was John's shirt, which was clearly hung for us to see. But nobody else was in sight.

"Why would John have hung his shirt there?" Marceline stated. I shifted my gaze toward her, my eyes full of worry.

"I—I kind of doubt John was the one who did that," I replied softly.

Understanding what I was implying, Marceline cupped her mouth with her hands and gasped.

"Now it's time to call the police," I said. We ran toward the nearest telephone, and I remember watching Marceline's fingers shake as she struggled to dial the three digits.

"Hi—I—I have an emergency to report," my roommate stuttered into the phone. "My friend walked across the street to tell our neighbor to stop staring into my apartment at night, and I—I think our neighbor might've attacked him."

Their short conversation became a vague blur, but Marceline soon informed me that the station had dispatched someone to check things out.

A bit later, there was a knock at the door; two officers had just finished a visit with our neighbor across the street. According to their discussion, the man denied any of our accusations. Aside from claiming to know nothing about John, he acted oblivious to ever having stared at any of us from his window in the first place. Of course, it's not like that behavior was rare for a psychopath, but we didn't like how the police officers seemed to believe everything he said and distrusted Marceline and me as a couple of spoiled rich kids.

I remember feeling very insulted by that, for some reason, and I wanted to share my whole life story to express that I was anything but an entitled brat. But it was no use; before we knew it, the officers were back on the streets, dealing with more "serious matters," as they liked to call them.

As frustrating as that interaction was, things intensified about an hour later when there was another knock at our door. Initially, we figured it was either John—or even the police, handing us a ticket for abusing their services with fantastical claims—but it was neither. It was our neighbor from across the street.

He didn't hesitate to welcome himself inside, and Marceline nor did I attempt to prevent him from doing so. He was much taller and even more intimidating than either of us had imagined him to be, so his appearance stunned us in several ways. His sudden appearance had a way of asserting that he was in control, and the fear made me feel as though I had lost most control over my muscles. Immediately, we could tell that the guy was irritated.

After he stepped inside our apartment, he shut the door behind him and started lecturing us about how foolish it was to send the police to his home. He stated that it was dumb enough to tell our friend, John, to confront him, but summoning the police took things to a new level of stupidity. He explained that there are things in our world that the police have no jurisdiction over and that it's best, for our sakes, that Marceline and I cease to continue spying on him from our apartment window.

Marceline became outraged by that statement, claiming *he* was the one watching *us*, but he quickly shut her up by aggressively stepping toward her. None of what the strange man said made much sense to me, but he did seem to genuinely believe that we were the ones watching him rather than the other way around. The primarily one-sided conversation was utterly bizarre. His tone made it seem as though we were entirely the ones to blame. But then he confessed to something upsetting.

"In any case, your friend was quite tasty," the man said in a very psychopathic way. His eyes twitched in strange directions as he revealed that information. It seemed like he went from playing things cool to losing control and could no longer resist telling us something that would deeply disturb us. Marceline didn't seem to believe any of it; she was just in denial. I, on the other hand, *did* believe this guy. I could immediately tell that he was as sociopathic as they came. And, on top of that, what was he exactly?

"What are you?" I couldn't help but ask as he stepped deeper into the apartment. Although I wanted him to leave more than anything, I was worried that we were about to experience gruesome deaths, but I had hoped I wouldn't have to do so without getting some answers.

"What am I?' he asked. "Well, let's just say I'm someone who should be treated with absolute respect— someone who could cause terrible things to happen to you and your loved ones. Unless you're looking to provoke me, I strongly encourage you to avoid sending the police to my home again—for any reason at all."

Marceline and I went speechless. We were terrified beyond comprehension. Everything was silent for around ten seconds as the man shifted his gaze back and forth between us. Suddenly, right before he turned around, a split, lizard-like tongue extended from his mouth before quickly retracting. He then proceeded to open the door and exit the apartment, winking before shutting it all the way.

There were probably about another thirty seconds that went by before we felt comfortable enough to utter even a single word.

"What—the—hell?" Marceline finally murmured with her eyes still on the door. I then noticed tears in her eyes; clearly, neither of us had expected that encounter or to receive death threats.

Marceline called her parents to inform them of what had happened, but she left out many of the disturbing details due to fear that our creepy neighbor might somehow find out. If everything he said was true, and he was connected to a group of people (or whatever they are) who are pretty much untouchable, who can say what they're capable of? Perhaps they can easily acquire transcripts of every phone conversation.

Anyway, Marceline's parents took their daughter's concern seriously enough to book her a Caribbean vacation to help her destress and get her mind right. They even booked a ticket for me since they probably didn't want their precious daughter traveling alone. I was lucky they were willing to pay for all that for me, for I probably would've been too scared to stay in that apartment alone for the next week.

When we returned from that vacation, they had already started remodeling the building across the street. I doubt there was any correlation to what we experienced; nonetheless, the timing was still interesting. Marceline never heard from John again, nor did we reencounter our neighbor from across the street. I only lived in our apartment for about eight more months after the terrifying confrontation because, unfortunately, Marceline became too much for me to handle. She turned out to be a lot more drama than I had anticipated, and it started interfering with my studies. By then, I had met another student from my school who needed a roommate, and I jumped at the opportunity.

I'll never have any idea if that creepy neighbor was in that condo across the street during the remainder of my time in Marceline's apartment, for the ongoing renovation construction obstructed my view of the windows that enabled us to spy on him before. I'm hoping it also disabled his view of us, but who knows?

A part of me wants to know if the man was sincere when he mentioned that he was untouchable from the authorities. If that was the truth, and he wasn't merely trying to intimidate us, it genuinely worries me to think there are people out there that the law can't punish. The concept that there could be differing rules for him and common folk like me is deeply unsettling. I hope he was merely bluffing when he mentioned that. Regardless, I wonder what that guy was. Was he originally an ordinary human who contracted some rare illness, or was he something else? I've always been curious to know the details, but I'm also worried that the truth could be overbearing.

THEM: They Come at Night, Volume 2

Are you enjoying the read?

I have decided to give back to the readers by making the following eBook **FREE!**

To claim your free eBook, head over to

www.LivingAmongBigfoot.com

and click the "FREE BOOK" tab!

Report #2

Delaware was one of the last places I would've expected to encounter a cryptid, especially one so rare. The experience taught me that we're likely never as alone as we think.

In 2002, I struggled through the most awkward time of my life. I was 29 years old, had recently separated from my wife—who I had dated since I was 20, and lost my job due to the company needing to scale back. Losing my career was perhaps the most devastating of all because I had imagined I had become indispensable to that employer. Aside from the founders, I had worked there longer than anyone else and knew the ropes inside and out.

Anyhow, it got to the point where it felt like I had hit rock bottom, and I knew I needed to do something to help climb my way out before there was no going back. I hate to admit it, but I was pretty close to that point of no return—if you know what I mean. Let's just say I had considered every option available.

One of the first things I decided to do was move to a much more affordable area. I had been living in Boston, a place where life was anything but cheap. It became apparent that temporarily living in a quieter, less populated area might do me some good. It was one of those periods that I think most people go through at some point. I knew I needed to implement change into my routine but wasn't sure how to go about it other than to relocate. It seemed like the only logical strategy that might trigger other unforeseen but positive changes. I just felt so dang lost.

I ended up deciding on a small town known as Arden. Well, it's more like a village than a town, which was a big part of why I chose it. It was a super charming place and seemed like a perfect place to temporarily move to so that I could reset my troubled mind. It's ranked as one of the safest places in the state, which is ironic, considering what I went through while living there.

I found the typical architecture of the village to have so much charm that I couldn't resist moving there almost as soon as I saw it for the first time. But since I had prepared to lose substantial money to my divorce, I wanted to find something extremely affordable. After having some trouble finding something in my intended price range, I met a woman at a café who told me her grandmother was looking for a renter for her house since she had recently moved to a nursing home. She didn't want to sell it because she insisted it remained in the family. But since nobody in her family wanted to pay the costly maintenance and taxes that came with it, she tried to find a temporary tenant to look after the place. I almost couldn't believe how perfect the timing seemed; it felt meant to be.

Those feelings of gratitude increased once I pulled up to the property; it was gorgeous, but it did need some upkeep. Fortunately, the woman's grandmother offered me an unbeatable rate in exchange for taking care of simple tasks like mowing the lawn, replacing lightbulbs, etc. Trust me when I say it was a no-brainer of a deal. I would've been a fool to consider rejecting the offer—or so I thought.

Everything at the rental property started nicely. Although I was still enduring a whirlwind of emotions, I at least felt like I had some room to breathe. The house sat on about four and a half acres, so I spent a lot of time strolling the yard, checking for things that might require maintenance. I didn't want only to do the minimum that the owner required; I wanted to come up with other projects that would lead to outcomes we'd both appreciate. One of the first things I thought of was to build a few hummingbird feeders. The property looked like one that would attract those little guys, but I had gone days without seeing a single one of them.

It immediately became evident how much moving to that place helped distract me from all the recent, ongoing turmoil. There were times throughout the day when I still had to acknowledge all of that negativity, but moving to Arden seemed to equip me to deal with it with a clearer head. I didn't even realize how badly I needed that until my perceptions were less clouded.

Everything felt like it had started on the right track. But, one night, a little over a week after I had moved in, something unexplainable occurred. I woke up around 2:00 to relieve myself and stepped on something sharp as I exited the bathroom. Wincing from the pain, I flipped on the light to get a better look at the floor and found a nail in the middle of the doorway. I can't express how surprised I was by seeing that object there.

I may have been guilty of many things during that time in my life, but being messy wasn't one of them. I've always taken pride in having an extremely organized living space, and my new rental property was no exception. Even if I had missed the object lying on the floor, what are the chances it would've sat pointed upward to puncture my skin? To say I was baffled by the whole thing would be putting it lightly. Fortunately, I had only stepped on the item with one of my smaller toes; otherwise, it could've easily pierced my entire foot.

I remember having a bad feeling as I cleaned the wound and bandaged my toe; it felt like someone was watching me inside the house. For peace of mind, I turned on every light inside the house and double-checked I had locked all the doors. Everything was secured, and I found no trace of anyone entering the home.

I then wondered if someone from the family, who had a spare key, didn't like that I was living there. Was it possible that one of the family members snuck inside in the middle of the night and planted a sharp object for me to step on? I knew that was such an absurd theory, but if you were as much of a clean freak as I was, you would understand why I would start thinking of potentialities like that. I knew I wouldn't have left that nail there—especially erect. I couldn't think of any other possibilities.

But by morning, I felt significantly better and wrote the incident off much easier than during the previous night. Since I had thrown the nail in the trash, I tried to look at it like it was nothing more than a strange dream. Of course, I was still confused, but I didn't want to spend time dwelling on something I likely wouldn't get to the bottom of.

After getting ready to go to the hardware store, I walked outside and found several bird skeletons on the way to my car. Four were laid out in a perfect line, each around half a foot apart.

"What the hell?" I gasped. In addition to them laying in an orderly row, every feather and ounce of meat had been picked clean. That made it difficult to believe that it was the act of a typical woodland predator; this was performed by someone or something intending to intimidate me.

I began to wonder if there was some teenager in the family I didn't know about, looking to make me feel unwelcomed so that they could get a good laugh or something. Truthfully, that's what I wanted to believe, for every other potentiality I could think of felt far more threatening. Whatever was going on, it felt evident that someone was acting maliciously toward me, but why? Aside from the conflict with my wife, I didn't have problems with anyone. So, why would anyone target me?

    I don't know how long I stood there, examining the bird skeletons, but I was unsure how to proceed. I wondered if I should dispose of the bones by tossing them beyond the tree line or just let them be. A little part of me felt inclined to disregard the recent oddities, for I didn't want to make it look like I was intimidated in case someone was watching. Although I thought I got a great deal, I paid a significant sum of money upfront to negotiate the best possible price; I didn't know whether getting a refund would be difficult if I decided to break the lease.

Eventually, I continued toward my car without touching the skeletons and headed for the hardware store, wanting to carry on with my day. When I returned a few hours later, the remains had vanished. Still, I tried not to think too hard about it, assuming that a scavenger had taken them elsewhere.

Later that afternoon, I was preparing to cut the grass when I heard footsteps in the nearby wood line. It seemed like someone was tiptoeing atop fallen leaves, but the dense vegetation obstructed my view of them.

"Who's there?" I called out.

There was no response.

"I know you put that nail in the house last night and laid the bird skeletons on the ground. You better stop those games unless you want the police to get involved."

I wasn't sure that there was actually someone walking around out there while I said all that, but if there was, I wanted them to know I was aware and that I wouldn't take kindly to more antics. But again, no one replied to me. The sounds of footsteps stopped, leading me to suspect that if there was someone behind the tree line, they had found a perfect spot to watch my every move.

I didn't want to make it look like I was intimidated by anyone, for I felt that would encourage them to keep messing with me, but I also didn't think it was a great idea to stick around out there with someone potentially watching me while I couldn't see them. So, I decided to continue with whatever I was doing for a bit longer, attempting to appear unconcerned.

Eventually, I headed back toward the house, and that was when I saw the set of eyes staring at me from inside. They appeared closer together and low to the ground, making me assume it was a teenager that had been playing pranks on me.

Without further hesitation, I rushed inside, knowing I needed to take charge if I ever wanted this crap to end, hoping I'd be able to acquire the phone number of the kid's parents and ensure they were grounded or punished in some form. To make a long story short, I had dealt with a group of disrespectful teenagers in the past, so I had assumed this would be no different.

After practically kicking the door down, I instantly felt the strangest sensation to date. My muscles went completely still after making it no more than three or four feet inside the house. Not only did I freeze up, but I quickly started to get an awful cramp-like sensation in my right hamstring, causing me to wince. I wanted to grab it or change my position so badly, but it was no use; I was paralyzed.

I couldn't believe my eyes when the strangest of beings slowly hobbled into the foyer from around the corner. I could tell it was a male, but I couldn't tell what it was; it wasn't a human, but it walked a lot like one and had humanlike expressions. Whatever it was, it got closer and closer until it was inches away. Every ounce of me wanted to escape the intruder, but I couldn't even utter a word. The only thing I could move slightly was my eyes, and they even had trouble matching the careful pace of the strange creature's movements. Its space reminded me of how some movies depict elves, only much creepier and more sinister. I couldn't believe any of it was happening.

As the thing circled me, I observed its spiky back out of my peripheral vision. It reminded me of what you would see on a hedgehog or a porcupine. Even though I couldn't look at it with complete focus, I was sure it was an extension of its torso and not part of some outfit.

The short intruder must've circled me at least four or five times, occasionally muttering things that didn't make sense to me; it easily could've been a different language but was spoken too softly to discern. I was under the impression that it was analyzing me and deciding what to do with me. Whatever was going on, it felt apparent that this thing didn't appreciate my presence; it was no friend, that's for sure.

There was a point when the intruder got closer behind me and started sniffing my lower back. The sounds of that made it seem much wilder and feral. I would say that that solidified the notion that this was no human I was dealing with; it was some rare creature.

It was incredibly aggravating how I couldn't utter a single word while I wanted to tell the creature to get away from me and possibly do something to intimidate it. I can't imagine a more frightening scenario than being entirely at the mercy of some creepy entity I've never seen or heard of before. I would've preferred to be in front of a hungry grizzly bear and have governance over my muscles than be with that strange intruder, unable to move or speak. I can't imagine another scenario where I would feel as vulnerable as I did during this event. It was horrifying.

Since I knew nothing about the entity, I had no way of knowing whether it was doing something to me at that moment or if there might've been something on that nail that I stepped on, which was slow to activate. Either way, I worried that, even if I survived this encounter, I would be paralyzed for the remainder of my days. Feeling panicked and frightened while unable to defend yourself leads to a whole other excruciating experience.

It felt like I was nearing a peak of internal insanity when I suddenly could move again. My body sprung forward uncontrollably after a long period of desperation to escape the intruder, and I fell to the floor face-first. I immediately rolled over onto my back, expecting that the intruder had accidentally allowed me to regain control and was likely about to attack. However, nothing was there; I appeared alone in the foyer.

With my heart palpitating, I rose to my feet, rapidly checking every direction, still expecting the intruder to ambush me. But soon, the house and interior began to feel calm, which quickly helped me to feel slightly more relaxed, regardless of the unexplainable event I had just suffered. When it became evident that the coast was clear of that mysterious menace, I found myself confused about what to do; honestly, how is anyone supposed to proceed with their day after something like that, let alone the foreseeable future?

After sneaking into the kitchen and grabbing a giant butcher knife in sight, I carefully searched every room in the house. Since I hadn't heard any doors open or close following the encounter, I was fully prepared for the intruder to be hiding in one of the rooms or closets. But I found nothing. Not only had I not located the mysterious creature, but I also found no trace of it. There were no nails, bird bones, or other creepy objects in areas I might occupy throughout the day.

Once I began to feel more secure, I took the portable landline telephone outside with me. I wanted to call the family member who had handed me the lease agreement, but he seemed like a bit of a hothead, and I felt he would deny my story even if he knew something about it. After careful thought, I decided to drive to the coffee shop, where I met the barista who referred me to the rental property in the first place. She came off to me like she would be far more understanding during difficult conversations, and I felt she would be the best candidate for not immediately dismissing me as crazy. Even if she thought it, she would probably keep it to herself.

When I arrived at the coffee shop, I was disappointed not to see her behind the counter. I asked one of the other employees, and they informed me that she wasn't scheduled to work that day. However, as I exited the café, I crossed paths with the individual I was looking for, and she even recognized me.

She explained that one of her associates asked her to cover their shift at the last minute, and she agreed to do them a favor in exchange for their help in the future. I wanted to ask her to walk with me so that I could explain my horrifying experience; however, I felt that might come off as a little creepy since she barely knew me, but we ended up grabbing a table inside for a few minutes before she had to work.

The poor girl looked shocked by everything I told her, but then she mentioned that other family members had said they thought her grandmother's house was haunted. She didn't go into much detail nor claimed to have heard anything about the specific entity I encountered. Still, she admitted the property was known by her family and their close friends for strange occurrences. But she hadn't spent the night there since she was a small child, for whatever reason, so she hadn't personally dealt with any of the phenomena.

One thing led to the next; eventually, I spoke to the grandmother directly. I almost couldn't believe my ears when she apologized for my experience. I thought she would've said I had to have been imagining things, but she was very sympathetic. Her reaction made me feel two very distinct emotions. In one way, I felt reassured, given that I had confirmation I hadn't lost my mind. On the other hand, I didn't particularly appreciate having it confirmed as a reality; I think I would've preferred to discover that an encounter like that wasn't possible.

Although the older woman didn't seem to understand much about what had approached me, she did have a name for it. She referred to him as Oscar, and I don't know if she gave him that name or if he ever introduced himself as that. Either way, it's incredibly creepy. The homeowner didn't seem too terrified of the creature; however, I did get the impression that she found it hard to deal with; it was like she knew he had a short temper.

I want to know why anyone would rent their house out if they knew an entity like that came around frequently. That seems pretty irresponsible if you ask me. Fortunately, I got my money back, and I had other family members help me move my few heavy items out of there. I noted how nobody else wanted to talk about the subject, leaving me to wonder if they believed in it or if they wanted to avoid the topic for some reason. It's all so mysterious.

I was the one who had to search for an explanation, eventually learning of a cryptid referred to as a *Pukwudgie*. I had never heard of it before, but apparently, there's an entire species of these things and many unsettling historical events connected to them. Some articles stated that they might've been friendly toward humans once upon a time but aren't anymore. I can't verify how much truth there is to everything about them on the internet, but I was pretty surprised by how much information is available to the public.

There are a lot of opinions on the creatures that come off as pretty fantastical, in my opinion, but I suppose I'm not in a place to be critical, given what I went through in Arden. That encounter even made me question whether magic is real. According to people on the internet, it is, and *pukwudgies* harnessed it long ago. As crazy as all of it must sound, I'm not sure how else the creature could've disabled me at will and let me go soon after. What did it want from me?

Report #3

Hello, I'm Mike. When I was seven years old, we went on a family vacation in Idaho, where we experienced quite a scare. But it also gave birth to a new shared interest, bringing us closer.

My dad had always been a passionate fisherman. It was a tradition for us to go at least once nearly every weekend.

He ran a construction company while I was growing up, so I'm sure any activity in nature brought him much-needed solitude after listening to noisy, heavy machinery throughout the week. There was nothing that that guy looked forward to more than our annual summer vacation, where he usually got about ten days off from his job. We lived just outside Boise, and he and Mom always chose a destination within a driving distance of five hours or under. There was so much to explore in our home state that they figured they never needed to venture elsewhere.

In the summer of the encounter, we went to Kamiah—a place known for its gorgeous rivers. My parents rented a waterfront cabin, and we immediately started having a blast. The weather couldn't have been more perfect, so we barbecued over the firepit the first night of our stay. But while we were enjoying our food, we heard an odd noise coming from across the river. I immediately got scared because it seemed to catch Dad entirely by surprise. He mentioned how he had never heard anything like it. I'm unsure how to describe the mysterious noise, but it sounded like someone yelling, "Ooooohhhh-wop!"

The noise repeated several times before my dad, having had a couple of beers, attempted to mimic it.

There was a pause of silence.

A few moments later, the noise occurred two more times, back-to-back.

Dad quickly performed his best imitations, overwhelmingly curious about who or what was responsible for the noise.

"Roger, maybe we shouldn't—" Mom had begun to say apprehensively. Suddenly, a series of loud splashes erupted from the water in front of us.

I only glimpsed the large black shape, charging through the water on all fours, before my dad scooped me into his arms and rushed toward the house. It was undoubtedly the scariest moment of my life. There was just enough moonlight to make out what looked a little like a buffalo with a man's head. I think I only thought of it that way because it ran at us on all fours and had a hump on its back, which reminded me of a buffalo's shape. I only got to examine it for a few seconds before we arrived inside the house and locked the door.

We left the following morning and spent the rest of our vacation in Jackson, Wyoming—a significantly more populated place. We were all pretty scared during that previous night, but we suspected that the animal—which had to have been a sasquatch—did nothing more than a bluff charge. My parents were under the impression that it didn't appreciate my dad's attempts to mimic its mysterious calls.

The three of us became fascinated with sasquatches and have attended numerous conventions/conferences throughout the northwest. Sometimes, the reality that those creatures are out there still slaps me across the face. No matter how many times I acknowledge that the species is real, I doubt I'll ever be able to accept it fully. It sure is an exciting world we live in.

THEM: They Come at Night, Volume 2

More Free Books at My Digital Store

If you're looking for NEW reads, check out my digital store www.TomLyonsBooks.com.

Buying my books directly from me means you save money—because my store will always sell for less than big retailers like Amazon, Kobo, or Barnes & Noble. My store also offers sales, deals, bundles, and pre-order discounts you won't find anywhere else.

Visit my store now to check out exclusive books and other products not available anywhere else!

Report #4

Hello, Tom. My name is Mike, and I hope you'll find interest in my paranormal story.

I grew up with stringent parents in the 50s, and it never ceases to amaze me how much family-living standards have changed in this country. Those were indeed different times. Every weeknight, my father would come home after work and expect my mother to serve dinner no later than six. If she didn't place it on the dining room table by six on the dot, he would get out of his seat, put on his coat and hat, and head for the local pub. At least, that's what he always said he was doing. I was, of course, too young to go check things out for myself.

On those tense occasions when my father would leave the house due to dinner not getting served promptly, I would peek around the hallway corner to watch him put on his jacket, followed by his top hat, and he'd leave without saying a word. I would then have the displeasure of watching my mother cry, which always saddened me.

"What's wrong, Mommy?" I would ask.

But she would always respond with something short like, "oh, it's nothing, Dear."

Crying in front of me embarrassed her, and she always tried to toughen up if she discovered I was observing her during those depressing moments. At the time, I didn't understand quite how miserable those moments were for her. How could I have been? The worst things that had yet to happen to me were scraping my knee or accidentally breaking a toy.

I was so young and inexperienced that I figured you get over things after a short period, and often, it'll start to feel like they never even happened in the first place. But I believe that many of the conflicts between my mother and father stored a different type of tension in our house—energy that would last well until well after they were gone.

    Since I was an only child, I automatically inherited the house after my mother passed. Before that point, I never thought I would want to keep it. It felt outdated and needed too many renovations to make it a comfortable living environment and hold any future value. However, my wife, Judy, was much more interested in the house than I expected. And she convinced our young kids, Evan and Olivia, to also take a liking to it. Judy got everyone, aside from me, all enthusiastic about a renovation project. It's humorous that they all ganged up on me, trying to convince me how to spend *my* hard-earned money. Well, they succeeded!

I was a bit resentful toward my family for pressuring me like that (although I probably didn't show it). Still, I remember feeling happy that I surrendered to their wishes almost as soon as we started the remodeling process. Something about it made me feel like I was ridding the house of some stored tension and giving it new life. We added wood floors in every room and increased the size of the windows in the family room, kitchen, and master bedroom, enabling a lot more natural light to come in.

We took out nearly every bit of the old furniture and implemented more of a minimalist style, immediately making it feel like there was much more room to breathe. I remember feeling immense satisfaction the first night our family spent in the renovated house. It felt superior to our old home. Unfortunately, those feelings of joy didn't last.

    I'll never forget the night Olivia came into our room, crying and claiming she saw a man in her room. Of course, my immediate worry was that some pervert had snuck into my daughter's room. The idea infuriated me. But I quickly calmed down when I recalled that we had installed a state-of-the-art security system, and there weren't many ways to break into that house. Undoubtedly, we would've heard someone come in because they would've had to break a window or something. In any case, I walked Olivia to her room to prove there wasn't anyone in there.

As I had expected, there was nobody present. I opened the closet, checked under her bed with her, and ensured that her window was locked. It was. My daughter continued insisting that she saw someone, but after spending a few more minutes in her room with her, I finally convinced her that she had dreamt it or that her sleepy eyes had fooled her.

It felt like I had returned peace to the house, but when I stepped back into the hallway, I got this awful, chilling feeling. It wasn't just as if the air conditioning was on in the hallway alone, but as if there was a temperature drop of about thirty to forty degrees; It was that prominent, and it gave me one of the strangest sensations I had ever felt up to that point in my life. Of course, I was aware that others had experienced temperature drops when paranormal entities were present, but I didn't yet believe in that kind of thing, so I disregarded it at the time.

After lying back in bed, I soon began to feel slightly uneasy that I had had Olivia return to her room. I didn't understand why, but I eventually assumed it was because I worried that she was frightened and having trouble falling asleep. I even considered getting her and bringing her back into our room for the night, but ultimately decided that that could set a bad example for the future. I didn't want her to think that she could flee her room anytime something caused her to feel scared; an expectation like that could easily interfere with my sleep, which was precious to me due to my busy life.

I felt relieved the following morning when my daughter told us that she hadn't again seen the man during the rest of the night. That reassured me that she had questioned her perceptions and might have gained some wisdom from the little mishap. Unfortunately, only a couple of nights later, my wife told me she had experienced something unsettling.

I was going over my legal work in my study when my wife rushed in and closed the door. She looked the palest I had ever seen her, signaling something was deeply wrong—especially given that she wasn't the type to spook easily. Those aspects alone concerned me before she even spoke a word.

"Please don't think I'm crazy, but I might have seen what Olivia was talking about the other night."

"Huh?" I replied, unsure how to handle the surprising claim. My wife wasn't the type to joke around about stuff like that, so I felt confident she wasn't trying to yank my chain.

"Are you serious?" I eventually asked, requiring confirmation that I had heard correctly.

My wife nodded. "This might be hard for you to hear," she continued, "but it looked a lot like your father."

There was a long pause of silence after she said that. I was already deeply confused by her words, but her belief that my father had somehow risen from the dead staggered me beyond comprehension.

"Honey—I'm not—I have no idea what I'm supposed to say to this," I stuttered.

Instead of saying anything else, my wife sat on a spare chair against the wall and began to cry, doing everything in her power to prevent the kids from hearing. I pulled up a seat next to her and spent the next fifteen minutes trying to console her as I did with my daughter. I attempted to persuade her that she was merely overly tired from all the busy work of renovating the house and looking after the kids. Unfortunately, my approach was a bad idea; everything I said seemed to frustrate her more.

"I know it's hard for you to hear," she said, "but I know what I saw. I can't explain how it's possible, but your father was there."

Not wanting to agitate her further, I decided to ask for additional details.

"Well, did he say anything?"

My wife shook her head. "He just stared at me in a way that made me feel he didn't know who I was. He looked upset—like he thought I had trespassed into his home."

"But then he left?" I asked.

"No, I was the first to leave the room," she said. "I then glanced into the kids' rooms to ensure they were okay before I came to you."

"And that was everything?" I asked, checking that I wasn't missing any details of what had occurred—or, at least, what my wife *thought* had occurred.

She nodded.

I yearned for something I could say that would make her feel better, but I was lost. All I could think was that we should both try to get a good night's rest and maybe try to figure out a way to understand more of what happened while sipping our morning coffee. She quickly agreed when I added how neither of us would want the kids to overhear any of what we had been discussing, as that could easily taint their view of their new home.

    While I was dosing off in bed, my wife asked me if there was any way I could call out of work the following day, for she didn't feel comfortable being the only adult in the house. I felt less at ease each time she mentioned what had happened in the kitchen. I don't know if it was so much that I worried there was a ghost in our house; I think it was more so that I wondered if my wife would ever feel safe in the home I had just poured loads of money into renovating.

    I wanted to do whatever I could to help her feel comfortable again as soon as possible, but my hands were tied. I had to attend an important deposition the following day that couldn't be rescheduled. Many busy professionals were working on the case, and it had been planned months in advance. My wife ultimately understood that there wasn't any way I could get out of it, so she came up with the idea to spend the day elsewhere and then take the kids to a movie after picking them up from school.

    I ended up being the first to arrive home the following evening, and it wasn't long after I popped open a beer and sat on the couch to turn on *Monday Night Football* that I noticed something odd in the TV screen's reflection. The visual was so unsettling that I couldn't help but lose grip of the remote before I could turn on the damn television. I'm not sure how long I sat there in silence, but it took my brain a long time to comprehend what I was looking at and accept that *he* was there.

"Dad?" I eventually asked, but my voice was strong enough for a mere murmur. He wore his top hat and coat, resembling how he would appear if he had just entered the house or was on his way out.

The figure in the reflection didn't say anything. Still, I felt an overwhelming amount of tension and that same chill I experienced in the hallway after leaving my daughter's bedroom a few nights earlier.

"Dad—is—is that you?" I asked.

There was another brief moment of silence before the entity resembling my father opened its mouth wide and made a noise that sounded like gurgling. Whatever that was, it was deep and guttural, and it seemed to shake my organs. I couldn't help but feel this awful sadness while unable to move. I might as well have been strapped to the couch; it was that powerful and debilitating. Then, suddenly, he vanished by turning and storming out of the room. I never got a look at the entity's feet, but it didn't look as though it ran out of view; it appeared as though it glided.

    I have no idea how long I sat on that couch, afraid to move a muscle, but I finally regained control when I heard the front door open, followed by the voices of my wife and kids.

    "What's wrong?" my wife asked as soon as we locked eyes; she could tell that something was up and already had her suspicions, given what she had been through the previous night. I didn't tell her immediately; instead, I asked if she had mentioned her encounter to either of the kids. She confirmed that she hadn't.

"Olivia?" I called out to my daughter after escorting my wife into the kitchen. After our daughter entered the room, I quickly checked that our son wasn't within listening distance. "Could you describe to Mommy and me what the man you thought you saw in your bedroom looked like?" I made sure to make my voice as pleasant as possible to avoid freaking her out.

"Um, he was tall—and—old," she replied while thinking carefully. "And—he had on a jacket—and a funny hat."

Neither my wife nor I knew what to say; we were too busy wondering how any of this was real.

"Okay, thank you, sweety," I said. "How about you and your brother do some arts and crafts in here with us?" Of course, I had considered that the kitchen was one of the places where the entity had appeared, but I still wanted the children to be in a place where we could easily keep an eye on them. I had no idea whether my father's ghost could harm them, but I didn't want to take any chances.

Since three of the four family members had encountered the entity, we deeply questioned whether we should stick around and wait for our son to see it too. My wife begged me to take us to a hotel for the night, and I quickly agreed. I craved a place to think everything through while not worrying about a ghost appearing out of nowhere.

After convincing the children that their mom and I felt like taking them on a surprise adventure, we put on a movie in their hotel bedroom and turned up the volume loud enough for them not to hear our discussion. That night, we decided we would list the house for sale. As much as we loved that home, we didn't want to deal with something we didn't even understand. Fortunately, due to the renovations, we sold the house for a better-than-expected price. It all ended up working out in the end.

My wife and I did our best to put our encounters with that entity behind us and move forward. We figured it was unproductive to dwell on something we wouldn't have to deal with any longer following the move. We moved back to our old town, which wasn't far away, and landed a great home with great energy, which we still own to this day.

There's no question that paranormal activity exists; I just hope ghosts or spirits—or whatever you prefer to call them—can't actually harm us.

Conclusion

Thanks for reading! If you're looking for more, be sure to read *THEM: They Come at Night, Volume 3.*

THEM: They Come at Night, Volume 2

Editor's Note

Before you go, I'd like to say "thank you" for purchasing this book.

I know you had various cryptid-related books to choose from, but you took a chance at my content.
Therefore, thanks for reading this one and sticking with it to the last page.

At this point, I'd like to ask you for a *tiny* favor; it would mean the world to me if you could leave a review wherever you purchased this book.

Your feedback will aid me as I continue to create products that you and many others can enjoy.

THEM: They Come at Night, Volume 2

Mailing List Sign-Up Form

Don't forget to sign up for the newsletter email list. I promise I will not use it to spam you but to ensure that you always receive the first word on any new releases, discounts, or giveaways! All you need to do is visit the following URL and enter your email address.

URL-

http://eepurl.com/dhnspT

THEM: They Come at Night, Volume 2

Social Media

Feel free to follow/reach out to me with questions or concerns on either Instagram or Twitter! I will do my best to follow back and respond to all comments.

Instagram:

@living_among_bigfoot

Twitter:

@AmongBigfoot

THEM: They Come at Night, Volume 2

About the Editor

A simple man at heart, Tom Lyons lived an ordinary existence for his first 52 years. Native to the great state of Wisconsin, he went through the motions of everyday life, residing near his family and developing a successful online business. The world he once knew would completely change shortly after moving out west, where he was confronted by the allegedly mythical species known as Bigfoot.

You can email him directly at:

Living.Among.Bigfoot@gmail.com